BODY LANGUAGE

Sarah Goldberg

Body Language

Sarah Goldberg

Table of Contents

Introduction

Body language is different from any other language known. It's not spoken, but once learned, it can tell you a whole lot more than what you just heard! In fact, over 90% of communication is not done verbally, but rather through non-verbal communication—body language. Learning body language is very beneficial; it can signal when someone is lying, angry, or genuinely happy. Our speech, although very important, doesn't really state how we feel all the time. Our body, on the other hand, is different, and although you can teach it a few tricks to fake some movements, our bodies will eventually always tell the truth.

This book will take you through five different common scenarios and break down a typical conversation viewed through the lens of body language dynamics. Although somewhat stereotyped, these basic conversations (talking with your boss, talking with someone on a date, etc) were chosen as they are typical conversations that people everywhere have every day. Utilize the exact methods and tips with each example given, and look for these patterns and behaviors the next time you have a conversation. A very helpful method is to have a conversation and then write down a few notes afterwards to help reinforce what you saw during the conversation.

Let's get started with a few pointers. To understand further what people are trying to say through their body language, you need to understand the three fundamental concepts below.

1. Do not base your readings on one gesture - look for clusters. You might talk to someone who repeatedly touches his nose; that doesn't automatically mean that he's lying. If the next thing he does is grab a handkerchief, then perhaps he merely has a runny nose. Also, look for cultural differences; gestures differ on how someone is brought up by their environment.

2. Look for congruence in the situation. The body is always aligned; hence if someone is pointing on the left but his eyes are looking the other direction, then something is definitely wrong and the possibility that what he's saying is not how he really feels is huge. What we say must always reflect what our body language shows.

3. Gestures should always be in the context in which way they occur. For instance, if the position of a person during a winter night includes shrugged shoulders with crossed arms and legs, then he's probably just cold rather than being defensive. On the other hand, if the person uses the same position, let's say, on a warm Sunday morning while you were talking, then perhaps what he's trying to say is that he doesn't approve of what you're saying or he's being negative.

4. Be subtle. Especially as you first start your analysis of body language during conversations, go slowly so as to maintain good flow of the verbal conversation whilst you observe the other person's body postures. You don't want to be starting at your boss's feet to see what she is trying to tell you with her foot position—she'll find it at best a bit odd and at worst she'll become upset with you! Learning body language and observing it effectively is a slow process and a learned skill like anything else. However, once you start observing these

patterns, it will be truly eye-opening and you'll become more and more effective at interpreting it.

Chapter One

Talking to Your Boss

When someone say the word 'boss', the first thing that pops into our heads is a superior, influential, and straightforward man or woman who, no matter how long you've been working with, is still fearsome. A lot of us still have problems approaching our boss even after working with them for years. To be honest, talking to your boss isn't really that hard - all you need are confidence and sometimes a little wit.

Some employees tremble at the sight of their boss and a lot are more worried in making a decision whether to approach their boss at all for fear that they might make the wrong move. Certainty is a very powerful tool here, if you can decipher your boss' mood and be certain of how he or she feels, then approaching your boss is not going to be a problem and creating a positive image for yourself is going to be a piece of cake. Knowledge is power and if you can read what your boss is saying through recognition of key body language indicators, you'll be a step ahead of everyone else!

The Handshake

Always notice your boss' gestures and postures. When giving a hand shake, bosses tend to give their hand with the palm facing down, making you accept it with the face of your palm facing up. Such a position eventually corresponds to you being submissive to him and him being superior to you. This however is very hard to reverse since superior people always compete for dominance and superiority, it would degrade their ego if they were the one to be submissive. So what do you to make even? What do you do to show that there's more to you than being just a typical, submissive employee? Next time, do a double grip: accept the handshake submissively but firmly, then use your other hand to handicap his hand, hence giving him the idea that you're not a sheep, that you have the will and confidence, and you have the audacity to prove it.

Eye focus

The eyes say a lot about a person; eyes are also an essential tool in body language. You can understand how a person feels through the direction in which their eyes are looking. This is also a good way to know how your conversation with the boss is going. If you're trying to be friendly with your boss and you notice that his eyes are somewhat glued to his watch or on his paperwork, change your strategy because it's a cue that your boss isn't interested in your presence. Another situation is if by chance, you're chatting with your boss on the hallway, or on the elevator, then you notice him looking at something else other than you, it's also a sign of distraction and disinterest. To say that a conversation is going well, you must see the other party looking at you with attentive eyes - a very common sign of interest.

Critical Evaluation and Hand-To-Face Gestures

The signal for a critical evaluation is the hand-to-face gesture. This position includes the index finger pointing up the cheek with another finger covering the mouth and the thumb supporting the chin. Further proof that a person is having a critical evaluation is when the arms and legs are tightly crossed, giving away a defensive and negative non-verbal statement. The next time you discuss a presentation with your boss and you see him or her in this posture, it's best to change your idea or politely dismiss yourself because when the boss says at the end "I'll think about it", what he or she is really saying is, "I don't like your presentation".

Mirroring

One of the biggest reasons that a lot of us fear our boss is how they make us feel inferior. To fight this, mirror the actions of your boss, but not mockingly or in a disrespectful way. Mirroring shows how close you are to a certain someone; two friends who are very close tend to copy each other's postures involuntarily - smiling, clapping, and so on. It is not a requirement for you to be already close to a person in order to mirror him, in fact, faking it when talking to an acquaintance tends to develop your relationship in a better way. So if you want to be close to your boss, mirror his or her actions: stand up straight, speak up with power, and believe that you are equals.

Superiority

Don't you just hate it when you enter your boss' office, start talking about a meeting or a presentation and then suddenly your boss clasped his or her hands and put them behind their head? This gesture states superiority. What your boss is actually trying to say is rather like boasting. This gesture typically means, "Ha! I'm so much powerful than you" or even, "Yes, someday perhaps when you become smarter than I . . ." No wonder even without saying those words directly, the action in and of itself annoys you! Next time, when you see this sort of gesture, mirror it, only then will your boss think that something is wrong, and then he or she will break from this position. Their next gesture would probably be a crossed arm - one that suggests inner defense!

Always remember to look for group clusters before deciphering someone else's body language. When talking to your boss, here are some possible scenarios and body signals that you might or have already encountered.

John is a very hardworking businessman; he worked at his company for five years. During the time being, he wanted to achieve a higher ranking, so he went into the boss' office to ask for a raise. The first thing he saw there was his boss, sitting on his high and comfy chair. John approached him quite trembling, and then sat on a chair next to the table. He doesn't know what to say, he crossed his arms and legs then he tapped anxiously on the folder he is currently holding - an obvious sign of nervousness and unpreparedness. The boss then asked him what he wanted but John just kept on stuttering words and avoiding his boss' gaze. The room was filled with dead air for a while until the boss stopped, clasped his hands together and put it behind his head, then he looked at John and asked if he went in to ask for a raise. John's eyes lit up because the boss finally figured out his intention. He also felt embarrassed thinking he might not meet the requirements - this attitude eventually destroys his confidence. When John was asked to show his company profile and achievements, he merely passed a folder containing his documents and sat silently as he looked at the boss scanning through it. The boss then handed him back his files; he touched his nose, rubbed his eyes and then he said, "John, I will think about it", then he offered John a handshake, signaling the end of discussion.

What could have happened if the body language was acknowledged and the approach was different? Here is an alternate version of the scene:

John is a very hardworking businessman; he worked at his company for five years. During that time, he wanted to achieve a higher ranking, so he went into the boss' office to ask for a raise. The first thing he saw there was his boss, sitting on his high and comfy chair. He walked to the boss' chair with a smile on his face, greeted the boss and complimented his tie, creating a short conversation. John now got the attention of his boss after they shared a good laugh. Then without further adieu, John stated his business - to ask for a raise. The boss asked for his company profile and achievements, John gave the documents; after scanning the files, the boss asked him a few questions, with confidence, John answered them gracefully as he accordingly copied his boss' gestures. The boss now felt quite easy with this fellow as he stood and offered him a handshake. Then he said, "John, I will think about it." John gladly accepted the handshake and left the office politely.

What were the simple body gestures observed? Didn't they create a different result?

Here is another situation:

Linda is a new employee and she strives to build a good relationship with everyone around her workplace. One day, during lunch, she met the boss in the canteen hallway. Taking this as an opportunity, she approached, greeted the boss and started a conversation. During their communication, Linda noticed her boss repeatedly looking at his watch, she knew what this meant but she continued talking anyway. To make matters worse, Linda talked about a lot of things that didn't really interest her boss; he responded while looking at other places except her - an indication of disinterest and boredom. When Linda's coworker John approached, the boss used this as an opportunity and immediately excused himself.

Here is an alternate version of the scene:

Linda is a new employee and she strives to build a good relationship with everyone around her workplace. One day, during lunch, she met the boss on the canteen hallway. Taking this opportunity, she approached, greeted the boss and started a conversation. During their communication, Linda noticed her boss repeatedly looking at his watch, she knew what this meant and as soon as she saw this, she immediately changed the subject until they stumbled upon something they both have interest in. Linda mirrored her boss and during the chat, and her boss then felt comfortable and mirrored her unknowingly as well. When her coworker John approached, the boss then dismissed himself politely and asked to talk again some other time.

Remember that your boss likes being a boss, being superior and being competitive - those are what build his or her image. In order to get on your boss's good side, you must balance being a good leader and a good follower. To submit too much will make your boss think that you're incompetent and unworthy of a promotion, or even the job. But to lead too much will make him or her think of you as competition for their own position, which may lead to you getting fired! You can't really say "Sir, I'm trying to prove my worth in this company but I am not trying to steal your position," can you? The best way to deliver this message then is through body language; if you can understand all of what your boss is trying to say - verbally and non-verbally, then it will be easier for you to create a lighter and more friendly atmosphere every time the two of you talk.

Chapter 2

Talking to Someone Else When You're on a Date

Males and females tend to differ in the way they understand and decipher things. According to recent research, women can understand body language better than men, and men can be subtler in being decoded than women. Let's take a look at some of the typical body language patterns seen in the dating scene to better understand this interplay between the sexes.

Crossed arms

A girl with her arms crossed is non-verbally saying that she's being defensive. She's not buying what you're saying to her! Women may intuitively sense that you're telling the truth but for whatever reason, this sign shows that they still doubt and choose to believe that you're lying. Fortunately, if you see your date in this position and you know that you're telling the truth, break her arms from crossing together--try making her hold a glass or reach for her hand, then you'll see that the body language message will change, the defensiveness and negativity will be broken! Jealous men also tend to react the same at the given situation and this strategy can also be used with them.

Opposing statements

One of the easiest gestures to tell if someone is lying is by the way they speak and if the context somehow opposes their action. For instance, if you explained to your date that you talked to another girl nearby because she was an old friend and then your date calmly said that she believes you, but as she says this, her head is swinging sideways - this actually shows that she's lying, and that she doesn't believe what you just said. Another example for girls is if you wanted to talk to someone and you asked your date to excuse you, he says that you're on a date with him and you shouldn't go, but as he say this, he was nodding, this in fact is a cue that he's allowing you to be excused - an opposition to what he just said. These are pretty simple examples, but remember that everyone has a "tell"—something to indicate that they are not telling the truth and this head shaking (which can be subtle) is a classic "tell".

Palm reading

When your date explains something to you with his hands opened and palms facing up, then believe your date because he's telling the truth. Open palm hands correspond to honesty; it's like saying "come at me, I've got nothing to hide". If on the other hand, he explained with his hands enclosed or shaped in semi circular pose, then he's probably hiding something.

Distracted look

While you chat with the other person, if you notice your date looking everywhere, the wall, the floor, his watch, or he's playing with the things near his reach, this indicates boredom and annoyance. Any minute now your date will ask for permission to leave, probably making some excuse that he needs to go home now. If you can spot this earlier, then dismiss the other party immediately, being left by your date is indeed a bad impression of you and an impolite way of treatment.

Fumbling/Tapping

When you see your date out of the corner of your eye as you talk with someone else, and you notice him fumbling or tapping, this indicates that he is being impatient, he might leave you any minute now. Dismiss yourself politely from the third party and return the instance you see this signal if you want to keep the feet of your date under the table.

Tidying up

As you talk to that certain someone, you notice that your date is tidying up - adjusting his tie, pulling his shirt/her dress and fixing his hair even when not needed, this signals insecurity. Commonly, men's magazines will try to tell you that, "if a girl is twirling her hair, she's interested in you". This is false! Your date is finding faults in themselves because of the attention that you're giving to them. When you see these clues, it's best to assure him that nothing is wrong and clearly express just that in whatever way you like - verbal or non-verbal. Furthermore, just focus your date as assurance that you're interested will give your date back their confidence.

Always remember to look for group clusters before deciphering someone else's body language. When talking to someone else when you're out on a date, here are some possible events and body signals that you might sooner or later encounter.

John is on a date with his longtime girlfriend. John excused himself for a while to go to the restroom. As he was about to go back, a girl approached him, and asked for the women's restroom. His girlfriend saw this. When he went back to their table, his girlfriend asked him who that woman was – he told the truth. But then somehow, his girlfriend didn't seem convinced as she crossed her arms and then later on, she fixed her hair and dress anxiously. A little while after they ate dinner and it was his girlfriend who went to the restroom this time. John meanwhile, while waiting at the table, met the woman once again. The woman thanked him this time and John welcomed the acknowledgement right before the woman left. Unfortunately, his girlfriend saw this as well and asked him what happened. With his palms faced up, John told her what took place. His girlfriend, (using an arm barrier) wasn't convinced. She sat down, but then after little while, she insisted that she just lost her appetite. Puzzled, John went home with his girlfriend but she didn't speak to him again that night.

What could have happened if the body language was acknowledged and the approach was different? Here is an alternate version of the scene:

John is on a date with his longtime girlfriend. John excused himself for a while to go to the restroom. As he was about to go back, a girl approached him, and asked for the women's restroom. His girlfriend saw this. When he went back to their table, his girlfriend asked him who that woman was – he told the truth. But then somehow, his girlfriend didn't seem convinced, she crossed her arms and then later on, she fixed her hair and dress anxiously. John noticed this and assured his girlfriend that nothing really is wrong; he reached for her hands - creating not only a romantic atmosphere but also offering a gesture of reassurance. A little while after they ate, it was his girlfriend who went to the restroom this time. John on the other hand, while waiting at the table, met the woman once again. The woman thanked him this time and John welcomed the acknowledgement right before the woman left. Unfortunately, his girlfriend saw this as well and asked him what happened. With his palm faced up, John told her what took place. Thinking fast, John reached for his girlfriend's hands, preventing her from creating an arm barrier and reassured her once again, he looked into her eyes and told her what she wanted to hear—that she was the person near and dear to his heart. His girlfriend then calmed down and they sat down and continued their meal. At the end of the night, John walked his girlfriend home and received a good night kiss.

What were the simple body gestures observed? Didn't they create a different result?

Here is another situation:

Linda is on a date with a guy she met online. They were talking and laughing and sharing their hearts out when a familiar face approached their table - Linda's old classmate. Linda welcomed him and due to her excitement, she talked and talked to him without realizing that she was on a date! Her date was making obvious signals--he fixed his attire anxiously and cleared his throat. Linda noticed this and she introduced the two guys to one another. When her classmate asked if he was bothering them, Linda said no and asked her date if her friend could join them. Her date responded politely and positively while he was swinging his head sideways. Linda took this affirmatively and invited her friend to join them. Linda's date finished eating first and then looked at different places to amuse him while the two were talking. Shortly after, he then dismissed himself and Linda didn't hear from her date again.

Here is an alternate version of the scene:

Linda is on a date with a guy she met online. They were talking and laughing and sharing their hearts out when a familiar face approached their table - Linda's old classmate. Linda composed herself and greeted him. She then introduced him to her date. Briefly, when Linda noticed her date making insecurity gestures such as fixing his hair and looking at different places, although she wanted to learn more about what happened to her former classmate, she asked for her friend to talk with her some other time and reminded him that she was currently on a date. Her friend understood this and left politely. Linda and her date ate and continued talking, laughing and sharing a long evening of conversation. They had a great time and her date caller her the next day to ask her out on a second date.

Chapter 3

Talking to Coworkers

Whether you're new or someone else is new in your workplace, it is best to develop a good relationship with everyone to create a more productive and lighter atmosphere at work. But how do you know if your coworker will like you? What signs should you look out for when talking to your coworkers?

Arm Barrier

A person who gives you an arm barrier the moment you approach is either nervous or being defensive. An arm barrier, as we learned previously, is a gesture where a person shields something in front of him - a bag, folder or his own arms - this posture can be translated to "What is he going to do to me?" or even, "He looks nice but I don't really feel easy around him." When you see your coworker in this position, give them some time or change the topic. It goes without saying don't pick hard communication subjects like religion, gender, or politics when you're talking to them for the first, second, and third time either! Try starting lightly like "How's the weather?" Always ask open-ended questions because if you were to ask closed ones such as "The weather is good, isn't it?" the moment they answer "yes" the communication dies.

Territorial Displays

It is a human nature to be territorial at times. Never invade someone else's territory otherwise it might make them feel uneasy. Here's a pretty clear example that you may have witnessed before. You're talking to your coworker, having lunch on a square table - you sit on one side and your coworker sits directly across from you. Notice that every time you push certain things on his side of the table such as salt, pepper, or the paper towel holder, they react defensively - they might put out an arm barrier or cross their arms - this is in fact a negative response! Prevent yourself from accessing their territory; otherwise your simple business lunch might turn out to be disastrous.

Hands on Hips

When you notice your coworker putting their hands on their hips, this is an expression of dominance. Example: You're talking to your coworker on the hallway, then suddenly he puts his hands on his hips. Don't you notice that he seems more powerful and more superior? Perhaps you don't realize this is an expression of dominance, but even without knowing it, you'll display the opposite: expressions of meekness. You'll begin to lower your shoulder and perhaps shrink back a bit. Why do people do this? It's because of the feelings your coworker feels every time he does this – he feels powerful, especially if the topic discussed is something that really piques his interest.

Don't feel small every time this happens; instead copy him! This is one of the easiest body language displays to conquer with mimicry and this strategy works every time.

Palms Up!

Palms facing up convey honesty (we learned this in the dating chapter) - it can be translated to "I'm telling you the truth, I've got nothing to hide." If your coworker is stating how happy she to be receiving your gift and her palm is openly facing up, then she is being sincere; however when she says this with a smile but either her palms are facing down or tucked in her pocket, then there's something that she's not really telling you.

Toe facing

This is where your toes are facing where the interest is. Sounds simple enough, but its very subtle and a quick clue to see if someone is interested in talking with you or talking with someone else that's around you. Let's say you started a conversation with a coworker. As you go on chatting and communicating, you feel quite puzzled. He's looking at you intently but somehow you feel that he is not really listening. Why is that? Did you look at his feet? Were his feet facing the exit door? That would be a tell-tale sign that he wanted to leave rather than talk with you. Another situation is when you're with your coworker discussing work. His response to you doesn't connect and may not even make much sense. Why? Its because his feet are facing his boss, who he's trying to impress with his new project idea. How then to overcome this body language display? Again, a simple tactic works well in this instance. Try asking him "Are those new shoes?" By making that instant focus on the feet, his attention will be turned back to you. Try it the next time you notice this particular body language display—it works like a charm!

Always remember to look for group clusters before deciphering someone else's body language. When talking to a coworker or two, here are some possible events and body signals that you might encounter.

John is an average employee. One day, he saw a new coworker. He wanted to build a good relationship with this person, as they would share the same workplace for a couple of years and so he tried to start a conversation with him. First off, he greeted him with a friendly "Hello, how are you doing today?" The coworker responded with a smile along with an arm barrier. John started discussing work, but this unfortunately didn't interest the second person and his coworker also looked at different places around the room to amuse himself and his feet were even pointed at the doorway. John continued talking and hit a sensitive topic. Then John shared his opinion on this topic, but the coworker's arms were now crossed. The coworker then shared his opinion on the subject but John insisted on his own viewpoints. Although smiling at that point, the coworker started making statements with his palms closed. They both continued trying to prove each other's point until the light conversation turned into a heated argument.

What could have happened if the body language was acknowledged and the approach was different? Here is an alternate version of the scene:

John is an average employee. One day, he saw a new coworker. He wanted to build a good relationship with this person as they would share the same workplace for a couple of years and so he tried to start a conversation with him. First off, he greeted him with a friendly, "Hello, how are you doing?" The coworker responded with a smile along with an arm barrier. John saw this and he tried to make the atmosphere lighter by making a joke, and the coworker laughed although a bit awkwardly. Then John tried breaking the arm barrier by offering him some water and showing him the water fountain. The barrier was broken and John tried copying his coworker's gestures to help stave off any superiority signals his coworker might be sending. John talked about light topics such as weather and sports until his coworker found him to be an outgoing and comfortable type of person. They were both focused on one another, and became more focused when suddenly a sensitive topic was brought up. They both shared their opinions on this, but when the atmosphere began to change, John immediately changed the subject and joked around to ease the situation. The coworker took the joke well and they parted on good terms.

What were the simple body gestures observed? Didn't they create a different result?

Here is another situation:

Linda is a new employee. During a company gathering, she was tasked to pair up with a coworker for a certain project. Linda approached her partner; she greeted her first then introduced herself - they were both only acquaintances at that point. As they sat down to work on the business project, Linda decided to have a short "getting to know you" chat with her coworker first. They shared some laughs during the chat but along the way, the coworker repeatedly tapped on the project plan as Linda continued talking. She kept on talking even when her coworker showed signs of disinterest and irritation such as looking at different places and rubbing her neck. The coworker, in a polite manner, finally suggested that they should go back to work. Linda agreed, but during the planning, she kept taking everything as a joke as she was a bit nervous working on this new project. At that point her coworker had had enough and so she started acting quite serious and she sternly asked Linda to be serious about her work as well. Their actions towards each other from then on became quite awkward and uneasy and as a result, the work on their project suffered.

Here is an alternate version of the scene:

Linda is a new employee. During a company gathering, she was tasked to pair up with a coworker for a certain project. Linda approached her partner; she greeted her first then introduced herself - they were both only acquaintances at that point. As they sat down to create the business project, Linda decided to have a "getting to know you" chat with her coworker first. They shared some laughs but when she saw her coworker tapping on the business plan, Linda then focused on the project. She understood that her coworker is the type who is a type A personality and had a "nose to the grindstone" work ethic. Only during lunch breaks did Linda chat about any non-business topics with her coworker; during working hours, it was all business. During work hours, although they talked with each other, they only focused on their project rather than their own personal lives. As a result, their project was completed 3 days ahead of schedule and their boss loved it.

Chapter 4

Talking to Your Parents

Parents are naturally protective of their children. They want nothing security for their kids no matter their age. As their children mature, often times the interaction between grown children and their parents can be difficult but once you understand the non-verbal communication that your parents might be using with you, you'll be able to communicate with them far more effectively. Here are some of the signals that you should look out for when talking to your parents.

Closed palms

A closed palm implies a negative message, and one clear message in parent-child communication typically shown by the closed palm posture is disagreement. Think about when you were a teenager—you probably asked your parents for a new car, and your parents might have responded with this gesture. It indicated that they didn't approve of your idea. Think about this scenario the next time that you're having a discussion with your parents on a touchy subject and keep a watch for the closed palm message.

Eyebrows up

Eyebrows that are in a high position suggest happiness. One of the common misconceptions that some people have is that parents are hard to please. Although this may be true in some instances, you really have to look at your parents' facial expression to get a true idea of how they're feeling about you. The tone of your father's voice when he congratulated you on a recent job may not have sounded happy; but keep in mind that if you saw him raise his eyebrows, then he was probably, in fact, pleased with you. It can be difficult sometimes for parents to express their true feelings in words and tone, but the eyebrows are a key indicator of their true feelings.

Arm Barrier

We're back to arm barrier again. As with the other examples in this book, when you see your parents giving an arm barrier gesture when you ask for something, be prepared for rejection - this signal is a negative and defensive one.

Knee Point

Similar to toe facing, knee pointing can indicate that wherever the knees are facing, the interest of that person lies there - the only difference here is that knee pointing is conducted while sitting. If ever you want to talk to your parents and they gave you the time, but along the way they don't seem interested, then perhaps there's something else that's getting their attention. If you see, for example, your father with his knees pointing to the kitchen or the bathroom, then he's thinking about what's occurring in those rooms instead of focusing on you. The best management strategy here is to offer to go into the room that his knees are pointing to (unless it's the bathroom!) and then continue the conversation in that room where he'll be more focused on you.

Hand-to-face

This gesture is often seen in business negotiations. Sometimes, you do become a salesperson when you're negotiating with your parents about something that you want. For instance, you want their approval of your fiancé, so you state all of his or her redeeming qualities, and then you try to persuade your parents into accepting him or her. What you're then looking for is a position where their index finger touches their cheek and the other fingers covering their mouth and their thumb supporting their chin - this gesture is a critical evaluation pose. If you see this pose, your parents are saying, "No, I don't approve of your fiance." If you see your parents in this position, you should immediately say, "Before you make your decision . . ." or some other sort of conjunction-type phrase ("And another thing…." or "Did you also know…") and then state some more advantages or positive qualities. It doesn't always work, but the quicker you can break this hands-to-face pose with additional positive statements, the better chance you have of a positive outcome for yourself.

Always remember to look for group clusters before deciphering someone else's body language. When talking to your parents, here are some possible events and body signals that you might have already encountered.

There was a time in John's teenage years when he asked his parents for something; more specifically, he wanted to have his own car. In doing this, he confronted his parents first. With their palms facing closed and hands crossed, they still chose to listen to their son's proposal but from a very defensive position as John's track record for being responsible was very poor. Virtually ignoring that fact and his parents' financial problems, John insisted on having his car vehemently. When his parents explained why he couldn't have one yet, John stormed out of the room. Unfortunately (or fortunately!) for John, he never got the car, and this caused further strain in his relationship with his parents

What could have happened if the body language was acknowledged and the approach was different? Here is an alternate version of the scene:

There was a time in John's teenage years when he asked his parents for something; more specifically, his own car. In doing this, he confronted his parents first. With their palms closed and hands crossed, they still chose to listen to their son's proposal. During the middle of it, his parents explained why he can't have one yet. When this happened he noticed his parents' palms open and face upwards showing they had nothing to hide. He became much less confrontational and although he was really disappointed, he chose to understand the situation and didn't push his intentions. This made his parents happy as John usually was fairly argumentative. His parents formed a savings plan with John and they both saved money little by little, and two years later John got his car.

What were the simple body gestures observed? Didn't they create a different result?

Here is another situation:

In her adult years, Linda brought home her new fiancé for her parents to meet. She was a little worried since her fiancé was an artist, not the doctor her parents wanted her to marry. She introduced her fiancé but she quickly noticed that her parents were not listening to her; they kept on peeping into the kitchen. This annoyed Linda and she immediately jumped to the conclusion that her parents disapproved of her fiancé. She stated, "Well, we're getting married no matter what you think", grabbed her fiancé, and stormed out of the house. She didn't speak to her parents until the wedding, and it was an extremely stressful time in her life.

Here is an alternate version of the scene:

In her adult years, Linda brought home her new fiancé for her parents to meet. She was a little worried since her fiancé was an artist, not the doctor her parents wanted her to marry. She introduced her fiancé but she quickly noticed that her parents were not listening to her; they kept on peeping into the kitchen. Linda noticed this and immediately asked what's wrong. Her mother then stated that she was canning jam that afternoon and she wanted to be sure that the jars were sealing properly. Linda acknowledged this situation and she offered to go help her mother in the kitchen and left her fiancé with her father. She was able to reflect all of the positive qualities of her fiancé to her mother in a one-on-one situation, and she heard some laughter from both her father and fiancé in the living room. Success!

Chapter 5

Talking to Your Children

Educating your children is a very sensitive topic. In order to instill good habits, you must provide a good role model for them from a very young age. The way you talk to your children can affect how they handle relationships, outside or inside of the family. At a very young age, it can be very easy to determine if they're lying or trying to manipulate you. But as time passes, their strategy and reactions change. Here are some signals and body language patterns that you might see in your child while you're talking to them.

Eye Contact

The eyes are the windows to the soul and its commonly said that one can see someone's honesty through their eyes. But that is not always the case! There are some instances where expert liars can look at you in the eyes, focused and intent, and you might infer that they are telling the truth when in fact they are not. There are also some times when a person who naturally feels awkward looking into someone else's eyes is accused of lying when in fact, he is actually telling the truth. So, how can you identify if your child is lying to you? You can tell it by the way their eyes are turned. If they are a right-handed person and you asked them a question and then they turned their eyes upward and to the right, then they are lying. The same is true (albeit in the opposite direction) with left-handed people. On the other hand, if you asked them the same question and they turned their eyes upwards and to the left, then they're just probably trying to remember something. Another indication of lying is when your child either blinks too much or blinks too slowly. If you notice both the blinking and the eye turning, you can be absolutely sure they are not telling the truth. This eye contact strategy also holds true in some adults, so be on the lookout for it the next time you think someone is not telling you the truth.

Hand-on-mouth

An fairly obvious signal that your child is lying is when they immediately put their hands on their mouth after answering or saying a statement. The obvious routine usually disappears as they grow older, but the mouth touching is still there even in adults. Teenagers and even adults may touch their lips accordingly or cover their mouth with a finger or two - those are still the same lying signals that originated from childhood. When you see your child in this posture, ask him to tell the truth as they are most likely lying to you at that point.

Glazed eyes

Even when a grown up person gets excited or happy, their eyes become shiny and you can see a change in how their eyes appear - this is a natural reaction to excitement. You can learn what your children want by the way their eyes respond. If you tell them about teddy bears and how you're going to buy them one, the eyes might brighten up; but when you discuss politics and there's no reaction in their eyes then they're obviously disinterested.

Yes/No Head Gesture

This is another telltale sign to indicate how your child really feels. For instance, lets say you asked your child if he wants to sing a song with you and then out of politeness, he answered that he would love to. As he say this, you noticed his head swinging sideways - remember that this is because his body is saying how he actually feels, which in this instance is the exact opposite of his own spoken words.

Palms

As we saw in the previous chapters, the palm is also an indicator of someone's honesty. Often the mistakes some parents commit involve jumping to conclusions based solely on the tone of how their children respond to them. Read their palms—when you were talking with your childe, were your child's palms open? Then he's got nothing to hide and is accepting your conversation. If he then responds and he touches his chest repeatedly, your child's statements are coming from his heart; but when he responds with his palms closed, dig deeper, as your child might not be telling the truth.

Always remember to look for group clusters before deciphering someone else's body language. When talking to your child, here are some possible events and body signals that you might sooner or have already encountered.

John and his son went out fishing one day. During their activity, John noticed his son looking very distant and far away. He asked him what's wrong, then taking his hands out from his pockets, he answered that there is nothing wrong. Having his instincts tell him that his son is not telling the truth, John responded with a sharp tone of voice and he commanded his son to not lie to him. This startled his son, but John was only eager to know what's bothering his son. He asked his son again what was wrong. His son didn't answer and kept his hands closed and fists clenched. John was now irritated, and he kept up the questioning until his son burst out that he had failed a subject at school. His son then put up an arm barrier; John on the other hand, couldn't further contain his emotions and yelled at him, expressing his disappointment.

What could have happened if the body language was acknowledged and the approach was different? Here is an alternate version of the scene:

John and his son went out fishing one day. During their activity, John noticed his son looking very distant and far away. He asked him what's wrong, then taking his hands out from his pockets, he answered that there is nothing wrong. Having his instincts tell him that his son is not telling the truth, and seeing his son with open hands, he knew he could take the opportunity to have his son open up to him. Therefore, in a calm and gentle way, John asked his son if he really is okay or if something was on his mind. His son didn't answer and John gave him some space and time to think. A few minutes later, in a nervous manner, his son confessed that he failed a subject at school and quickly apologized with a tear in his eye. While his son was saying this, John saw his son using an arm barrier - he knew the boy was preparing for the worst. John composed himself and although deeply disappointed and surprised, he gave his son a hug and told him to do better next time which immediately changed the atmosphere of the conversation. They dug deep and found out that his son was having trouble with his multiplication tables, and John and his son worked out a way to help him practice his math more effectively.

What were the simple body gestures observed? Didn't they create a different result?

Here is another situation:

Linda's daughter wanted to talk to her for advice on her new boyfriend. Linda went into her daughter's room and talked to her. After her daughter had talked for a few minutes, Linda started talking about her own experiences - experiences that mostly didn't concern her child's current situation. Her daughter felt awkward and moved her knees to face the doorway and her hand started rubbing her neck. Even when her daughter tried bringing up her own problems, Linda still talked about her past experiences without stopping and listening to her daughter. Her daughter finally had had enough and told her mother that she had to make a phone call and left the room.

Here is an alternate version of the scene:

Linda's daughter wanted to talk to her for advice on her new boyfriend. Linda went into her daughter's room and talked to her and she kept silent, listening intently to her daughter's dilemma. When asked what she would do in that situation, Linda spoke up but the rest of the time Linda only listened. Firmly but lovingly, she held her daughter's hands, preventing her from creating any barrier so that her daughter could absorb her knowledge and advice. When she answered her daughter and gave her advice, she was able to give her daughter tremendous comfort. Linda's daughter appreciated this and showed her acknowledgement with a big, warm hug.

Conclusion

Body language is a key component of everyday conversations and I hope that this book has been useful in explaining some of the basic patterns and concepts surrounding this key element of communication. Remember that you must always look at body language patterns as a group in order to most accurately delineate the underlying message. Remember as well that you must be subtle in your observations—if your boss catches you starting at her feet instead during a conversation, she's not going to like it! Good luck with your newfound communication strategies and as you look for these patterns more and more, it will truly be an eye-opening experience into the new world of body language.

I encourage feedback on improving the book and any suggestions you have; send me a Tweet to my Twitter handle @SGoldbergBooks and I'd love to hear from you.

Additional Resources:

Video resources:

These videos are hosted on the educational website Udemy, an easy-to-use platform for online learning. All of the videos are taught by experts and after reading this book they can augment your learning and teach you even more about the secrets of body language.

Body Language For Entrepreneurs

Course Description

Do you want to have more business success? Mastering body language is the missing ingredient for many business owners. Nonverbal communication can not only help you be more effective in your business dealings, but it can also give you an added edge above competitors.

93% of our communication is nonverbal.

But we rarely think about our body language when dealing with clients, investors or at networking. We think about what we are going to say, but we don't consider how we say something. Research shows how we say something is even more important than what we say.

This course is made up of the 6 areas every entrepreneur needs and how body language can help you succeed.

Customer Relations:

- Building Rapport
- Successful Selling
- Winning Client Relations
- Customer Validation

Your Nonverbal Brand:

- Effective Networking
- Impactful Elevator Pitching
- Building Your Online Presence

Building Your Business Team

- Lie Detection
- Hiring
- Finding Great Partners
- Connecting with Colleagues
- Leadership
- Management

High Pressure Business Situations

- Fundraising
- Investor Pitching
- Public Speaking
- Negotiations

This course will teach you how to be more effective in all of areas of your business.

Body language will completely change the way you do business.

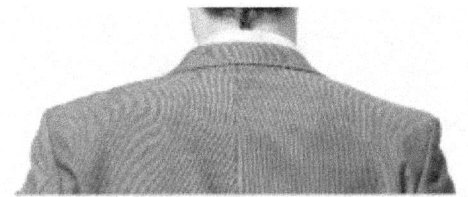

The Secrets of Body Language

Course Description

Do you ever wish you could know what someone is thinking? Body language is a great way to find out more about the person you are speaking with.

Perhaps you also wish you could improve your own body language or wonder about what your nonverbal behavior is saying to the outside world.

This body language course is based on scientifically backed research on the how to read people's nonverbal behavior and improve your own.

Whether you are a business owner, parent, spouse, employee, human resources director, teacher or student, this course will change the way you interact with those around you.

If you have ever interacted with another person, this course will be useful to you because our everyday interactions are filled with secret nonverbal cues just waiting to be uncovered.

Why Is Body Language Important?

Up to 93% of our communication is nonverbal. However, we often only think about the words we say, not how we say them. In this course, we will review the face, the body and how it expresses emotions and even talk a little bit about the lie detection.

In the Secrets of Body Language I give real life examples and tons of practical tips that you will be able to use immediately.

If You Don't Learn How to Decode Body Language Now, You'll Hate Yourself Later

At one point you will be on a date, in a business meeting, or in a negotiation and wish you know how to read body language. Invest the time in this course and you will be happy to have a leg up on your communication in the future.

If you wish you could begin to unravel the mysteries of body language, then enroll today in Secrets of Body Language now!

Book Resources:

The Definitive Book of Body Language

By Allan and Barbara Pease

We all know that what people say is often very different from what they think or feel. Now with Body Language, you can learn to read others' thoughts by their gestures. You can use it to tell if someone is lying. Find out how to make yourself likeable, and how to encourage cooperation from other people. You can use it in countless work situations, including how to interview and negotiate successfully. You can even use it to find a compatible friend or partner. Over half a million people have learned the secrets of body language with Allan Pease, and you can too.

This international bestseller reveals the secrets of nonverbal communication to give you confidence and control in any face-to-face encounter—from making a great first impressions and acing a job interview to finding the right partner. It is a scientific fact that people's gestures give away their true intentions. Yet most of us don't know how to read body language—and don't realize how our own physical movements speak to others. Now the world's foremost experts on the subject share their techniques for reading body language signals to achieve success in every area of life. Drawing upon more than thirty years in the field, as well as cutting-edge research from evolutionary biology, psychology, and medical technologies that demonstrate what happens in the brain, the authors examine each component of body language and give you the basic vocabulary to read attitudes and emotions through behavior. Filled with fascinating insights, humorous observations, and simple strategies that you can apply to any situation, this intriguing book will enrich your communication with and understanding of others—as well as yourself.

What Everybody is Saying: an Ex-FBI Agent's Guide to Speed Reading People

By Joe Navarro and Marvin Karlins

Read this book and send your nonverbal intelligence soaring. Joe Navarro, a former FBI counterintelligence officer and a recognized expert on nonverbal behavior, explains how to "speed-read" people: decode sentiments and behaviors, avoid hidden pitfalls, and look for deceptive behaviors. You'll also learn how your body language can influence what your boss, family, friends, and strangers think of you.

The Power of Body Language: How to Succeed in Every Business and Social Encounter

By Tonya Reiman

Nationally renowned body language expert Tonya Reiman illuminates what until now has been a gray area in interpersonal communication: harnessing the power of your nonverbal cues to get what you want out of *every* aspect of life, from professional encounters to personal relationships. Unlike other books on this fascinating topic, *The Power of Body Language* is your practical, personal playbook for getting what you desire from others -- and zeroing in on what others are saying to you without words. Once you know the hidden meaning behind specific gestures, facial cues, stances, and body movements, you will possess a sixth sense that can be a life-changing, career-saving, trouble-shooting skill you will never leave home without!

In an insightful and engaging narrative, Tonya Reiman analyzes all of the components of body language -- the languages of the face, the body, space and touch, and sound. She shows you how to become a Master Communicator with The Reiman Rapport Method, a surefire system for building an instant connection with anyone, in any situation. And she shares the experiences of her clients, from executives to politicians to relationship seekers: Learn from Cindy, a confident and ambitious manager who turned her career around by altering the subconscious messages she was sending her male colleagues...and Peter, the wedding DJ whose client list blossomed as soon as he practiced the art of social smiling!

<u>Body Language for Dummies</u>

Elizabeth Kuhnke

If you are puzzled by other people or want to improve the impression you give, knowing about body language could be the key. In this book you'll discover how the body reveals what people really mean and how you can use your body and your expressions to improve your self-image to others. It explores why we give the signals we do, how to read the most common expressions and goes on to show how you can use your new understanding of body language for success at work, in relationships and in your communication. Actions really do speak louder than words!

Communicate all the right messages – without saying a word! At any given moment your body is revealing more about what you're really thinking and feeling than your words ever could. Some people find this fact unnerving, but knowing how to read and control body language can be your key to success in life. Body Language For Dummies helps you become fluent in body language and to fine-tune your ability to read people and their mental states. Better yet, you can discover how to use your entire body to broadcast the right kinds of messages and to communicate more confidently, credibly, and persuasively. Let your body do the talking – see how the way you move and position your body can reveal inner states and affect how people see you, and observe how your thoughts, attitudes, and perceptions affect your posture. Read the signs – spot lies, notice subtle expressions of aggression, fear, or distrust, recognize signs of interest or rejection, and become more self-aware by observing your own body language. Understand how cultural differences can influence body language, and get wise with cross-cultural body language tips and taboos.

Online Resources:

http://www.stutteringhelp.org/7-tips-talking-your-child

http://www.sheknows.com/parenting/articles/814821/kids-and-communication-body-language-1

http://www.rightstartmagazine.co.uk/bodytalk.html

http://www.psychologytoday.com/blog/spycatcher/201004/body-language-essentials-your-children-parents

http://www.youtube.com/watch?v=sc_UWzHiUU0

Excerpt From "Toxic Relationships: Recognize A Toxic Relationship & Learn How To Fix It Or Forget It" by Sarah Goldberg

INTRODUCTION

Do you stare out of your bedroom window for no particular reason? Do you find it hard to maintain eye contact when you talk to people around you? Does it seem like you're hiding from the world? Are you sick and tired of the continuous pretense that your life seems to be these days? If these questions make you stop and think, then it would do you good to keep on reading. In the following sentences, you're going to unravel the truth behind your misery. This is exactly what Sarah did. Young, smart, intelligent and full of life, Sarah had so many possibilities ahead of her yet she chose to follow her heart. She was ready to tackle anything that life threw her way. Along came a charming young man, one thing led to another and Sarah ended up marrying him.

After just one year of their relationship she started noticing changes his behavior. These changes were along the lines of frustration with her, anger, and uncontrolled rage over trivial matters. Things started to go downhill from there. He started to degrade her and belittle things, ideas, and people that Sarah held dear. He liked to control every aspect of her life down to the kind of dresses she could wear. At first Sarah refused to see the situation for what it was because she was in denial, but as things started to get worse, she knew her relationship was now not satisfying but "toxic" in nature. She thought it was just a phase and tried her best to smooth things over, but she failed. After one year of living in hell with a man who considered her his property, to be used as he thought fit, Sarah decided she had had enough.

She took the first step by refusing to be a push-over. She realized that she had a life full of joy before she ever got married so she chose to fight and get it all back once again. She started to recognize the fact that if she didn't stand up for herself then her relationship with this man would destroy her personality and spirit. So, after gathering her courage and will power she sought out professional help as well as the counsel of her mother who then stood beside her in every decision that Sarah made. It was a long hard journey and she would often just curl up in bed and cry but the strong-willed girl didn't give up.

Today Sarah is a single mother of a very lovely son. She is happy, independent, and confident with her lifestyle and she is proud of the fact that she had the courage to stand up for herself at that time. She is engaged to Conner who loves her more than most guys love Monday Night Football! The courage that she managed to show three years ago not only helped her in saving herself from an abusive relationship but also secured a bright and happy future for her son.

Relationships are not always perfect regardless of whether they exist between spouses, siblings, business partners, or friends. They are more like a rough road fraught with ups and downs and to overcome them, both of the involved parties need to compromise so that they can move forward. However, it is easier said than done because more often than not people can't find the balance needed to sail a rocking ship and ultimately their relationships end in hurt and pain. This is where a thought like, "Am I in a toxic relationship?" originates.

A debilitated relationship also known as a toxic relationship usually refers to a relationship that drains you emotionally and physically instead of being a source of peace and contentment. Toxic relationships not only make you frustrated but they also take a toll on your spirituality, personality, and mentality. The loudest indicator of a toxic relationship is the increased level of suffering from stress. Lack of sleep, reduced appetite, avoidance, sullenness, forgetfulness, and anger are all symptoms of stress caused by a toxic relationship. Healing needs guidance, compassion, and compromise from both the parties to bridge gaps, fill voids, and repair the damage incurred by the dysfunctional relationship.

Untangling yourself from such parasitic relationships is never an easy feat. It demands a lot of courage and you have to stop being used. The most important step is to acknowledge the ground realities and work systematically to resolve issues. You need to take control of the life that you have repressed and ignored for so long, create boundaries, stand up for yourself, and don't feel ashamed about it because after all, you are only human. Consider your partner or sibling as your mirror and use what they reflect at you as your guide. Decide whether you can redeem your relationship and see if it is really worth all the effort. If yes, then go ahead and look for answers. If no, then go for a clean break and start fresh.

This eBook won't be a walk in the park for those of you who are going through rough times in relationships. It aims to stop you from running and face the music. It will make you question yourself and come to terms with your issues. However, one thing can be said for sure, by the time you're done reading, you'll have a solid plan to make your life easier and happier.

Like what you've read so far? Get the rest of this popular book on Amazon Kindle today by following this link.

Other Books By The Author

Banish Clutter: Simplify Your Life In Only One Weekend!
(#1 Amazon Bestseller!)

How To Deal With Manipulative People

Disclaimer

All attempts have been made to verify the information contained in this book but the author and publisher do not bear any responsibility for errors or omissions. Any perceived negative connotation of any individual, group, or company is purely unintentional. Furthermore, this book is intended as entertainment only and as such, any and all responsibility for actions taken upon reading this book lies with the reader alone and not with the author or publisher. This book is not intended as psychiatric or relationship advice and the reader alone holds sole responsibility for any consequences of any actions taken or not taken after reading this book. Additionally, it is the reader's responsibility alone and not the author's or publisher's to ensure that all applicable laws and regulations for business practice are adhered to. Lastly, I sometimes utilize affiliate links in the content of this book and as such, if you make a purchase through these links, I will gain a small commission.